Contents

Additional copies of
One Year Later—Remembering 9/11
(ISBN 083-412-0283) may be ordered from the
Nazarene Publishing House by calling toll-free
1-800-877-0700. Limited quantities necessitate restricting
orders to 10 complimentary copies per church. However,
electronic copies are available for download free of charge at
<www.usamission.org>.

ONE YEAR LATER . . .
Remembering 9/11

The Church Reflects and
Responds at Ground Zero

Edited by Tom Nees

Beacon Hill Press of Kansas City
Kansas City, Missouri

INTRODUCTION

One Year Later
Remembering 9/11

This is a thank-you note to thousands of Nazarenes who have prayed together and given generously to help the victims of 9/11 in New York and Washington, D.C. It's a compilation of reflections by our leaders and those serving in the trenches at Ground Zero.

In conversations with our general superintendents, it becomes clear that 9/11 has become a profound faith issue affecting not only the United States but also the whole world.

Volunteers preparing to serve through Nazarene Disaster Response surely did not expect such a tragic event, but they were organized and ready. Their eyewitness accounts of the activities at Ground Zero document the church's response and will continue to do so for months and years to come.

"One Year Later"—nearly everyone knows what it means. And we all remember where we were on the morning of September 11, 2001.

It has become a defining moment—life as it was before and life as it is now. The United States is at war—a war unlike any before.

We've grown accustomed to periodic warnings that further attacks are expected. Long lines at airports and sporting events alter our easygoing American way of life.

Our faith has been challenged. Terrorism in the name of God has forced people of faith to think more deeply about God. Christians have been called upon to explain as well as comfort.

During the past year, we've had time to think about what faith means. Books and videos are available to help us reflect and remember. More than 25 million copies of *Fallen but Not Forgotten*, a booklet published by Campus Crusade, have been distributed.

An extensive menu of resources is available at the web site <www.support.911remembrance.com>. The web site for Nazarene Disaster Response <www.nazarenedisaterresponse.org> contains information about the Nazarene response to the victims of terrorism in New York City.

And now, one year later, it is a time for reflection. Many churches will have special prayer services on Wednesday, September 11, 2002, and the following Sunday will become a National Day of Remembrance.

One year later we reaffirm the faith that provides us strength to withstand tragedy and grace to survive the threat of future attacks.

Tom Nees
Mission Strategy Director
USA/Canada Mission/Evangelism Department
Church of the Nazarene

PART 1

The Church After 9/11
Conversations with the General Superintendents

Tom Nees

Six months after 9/11, the general superintendents reflected on the implications of the terrorist attacks on New York and Washington, D.C., for the Church. Their six conversations were distributed via E-mail and can still be viewed on the USA/Canada web site:

www.usamission.org.

Each general superintendent observed two new realities. The world has changed. And the Church can never be the same.

How should the Church and Nazarenes respond? What unique contribution do people who embrace the Wesleyan-Holiness theological tradition have to offer? These were the questions that each general superintendent addressed.

Dr. Jesse C. Middendorf

> *In this first of six conversations, Dr. Jesse C. Middendorf states that the attacks in New York and Washington had international significance for the Church, as well as the world at large.*

How has the Church been affected by the terrorist attacks on New York and Washington?

It's obvious to me that the entire world was impacted by 9/11. The conversations that I have had with pastors in the U.S. since that day indicate that every church has been affected in ways that we had not realized at first. People are still discovering new implications of that fateful day.

It is the spiritual impact that provides the church the greatest opportunity. People are asking deep, serious questions about life-and-death issues. Priorities for many people were re-arranged, and spiritual issues have become much more central to our existence.

What are people wanting and needing to hear?

I think they want to hear that there is hope, that life has some meaning, and that God cares.

They now know that there are some things more important than some of the pursuits that preoccupied us prior to 9/11. And this goes far beyond national boundaries of the United States. I think that is the thing that has struck me so much. I have seen a deep reassessment of values in people around the world. This has caused people to ask a lot of ultimate questions.

What should the Church be saying?

I think the Church has to speak with a renewed authority of its hope in Christ. It seems to me that our message tended to be a bit apologetic before 9/11. At times it seemed that we were not as bold as we should have been about the fact that ultimately our only hope is Jesus. I think our quadrennial theme "Jesus the Hope" was most timely.

You have been with the Nazarene pastors of the Metro New York District early on and more recently. What do you sense from them?

I don't think many of them realized how tired emotionally and physically and spiritually they had become. The toll was heavy on those who spent weeks leading their churches through the inevitable adjustments that were so necessary. On the other hand, I heard many of them telling remarkable stories of people turning to God, of their churches coming alive, of a greater sensitivity to the needs of other people. Many people who lost jobs as a result of the attacks are still being assisted by churches across the Metro New York District.

How do you account for the generous response of Nazarenes in giving over $700,000 to help the churches in New York respond?

Well, it has been overwhelming. I think some of the stories of sacrifice that people made so that they could send offerings and gifts are remarkable—even from overseas. Some of the stories I've heard are from missionaries telling of people who wanted to send at least a little something to help their American brothers and sisters. I think our people have demonstrated a compassion that says something about the DNA of the Church of the Nazarene.

Our people are remarkably generous, and this has been demonstrated again in response to this tragedy. God is using that generosity to touch thousands of people across New York City. I am thrilled with what has happened. God must be pleased with His Church.

Dr. Jim L. Bond

> *Dr. Jim L. Bond reflects on the increased interest in Islam and other world religions since 9/11. Interdenominational and interfaith cooperation seems to be increasing. At the same time, there is evidence of religious intolerance in the U.S. and around the world.*

How do we build bridges to those of other faith traditions?

As world religions, particularly Islam, become increasingly aggressive, it does present a serious challenge to Christians. How do we address this issue made more poignant after 9/11? Not with fear, disrespect, or animosity. It is not our strategy to silence people of other religions through intimidation, argumentation, or persuasive logic. Our way of winning people to Christ comes from an entirely different perspective.

What is the most effective Christian witness?

It is the way of love—patient, kind, never rude, not-easily-angered love! Our goal in everything is to be like Jesus, even in the way we witness to Muslims. How would He respond to those who perpetrated the 9/11 tragedy? "Love your enemies and pray for those who persecute you" (Matt. 5:44). Love wins!

Love helps us build bridges to people of other religions. We must remember that these people, like us, are questing spiritually to know the true God—and God is at work in every human heart through prevenient grace. Acknowledging that all truth is from God, we must find places of mutual agreement that begin to break down barriers. Finding some common ground and trusting the Holy Spirit to guide us, we can anticipate that He will give us the opportunity to share, in love, the Christian distinctives.

How do you suggest that we do that?

We have to go to these people and be involved with them. All truth is from God. We need to find places where there can be mutual agreement. I think once we reach points of agreement with people we begin to break down barriers. We have to try to find some common ground and trust the Holy Spirit to guide us.

What place is there for belief in the truth as revealed in Jesus?

Amid the pluralism of today's world, we are uncompromising regarding the exclusiveness of

Christ. The early Christians resisted all efforts to syncretize the Christian faith. Their hearts were aflame with a burning conviction: "Salvation is found in no one else, for there is no other name under heaven given to men by which we must be saved" (Acts 4:12).

When he was the archbishop of Canterbury, Michael Ramsey was challenged by a man who said, "I don't like your exclusiveness. You say Christ is the only way to God." Ramsey replied, "I never said that. Jesus was the one who said that. Jesus was the one who made that claim . . . I am committed as His follower to teach what He taught." This statement must be our guiding light today.

Dr. W. Talmadge Johnson

> *A heightened awareness of mortality, threat, and fear has led many people to churches in search of a faith that will give them strength to survive uncertain times. Dr. Johnson sees opportunity emerging from the tragedy of 9/11.*

Where were you on September 11?

I was changing flights at Chicago Midway. It was at that moment that I looked at a TV monitor and saw the events unfolding. I made the trip back to Houston via Amtrak and bus—a 26-hour ride—and then rented a car and drove home on the following Saturday. I was in our home church on Sunday morning. I think we had one of the largest attendances on that particular day that we've had in Olathe College Church.

On one of the news networks, a national news commentator said, "The churches are filling up to the rafters." The churches had become a haven or a place of refuge. A place of hope.

Is there still the same kind of interest six months after 9/11?

I don't see it at the level I wish it were. However, I still think that there still is significant turning to God. In many respects, it may depend on us in the Church. This is an opportunity to intensify our own faithfulness and devotion to God. When I think about church attendance, I am drawn to Ps. 122—David's words where he said, "I was glad when they said to me, 'Let us go into the house of the LORD'" (v. 1, NKJV). It ends by saying, "Because of the house of the LORD our God I will seek your good" (v. 9, NKJV), or as Peterson paraphrases it, "I'll do my very best for you" (TM).

I think to some extent that, rather than building a focus just on fear and uncertainty, we ought to seize it as an opportunity to strengthen our own relationship with God. What does this say to the Church? Do we just run for help when the thunder is roaring and the lightning is flashing? How do we recognize that we are to be faithful under all circumstances and then be ready for the crisis?

I don't think the crises are over in our world. I'm looking at the news this morning hearing what's going on in the renewed skirmishes in Afghanistan and the anxiety about the threat of a bomb in New York City. People look back and ask, should the government have done this, or should the government have done that? Perhaps what we ought to be asking is, what should the Church be doing?

What should churches be doing?

I don't know that we have to be so innovative as we do to be for real—to connect with people. I've been drawn to the significance of the meaning of connection. In the aftermath, people can run but they can't hide from the reality. I think we should to try to demonstrate that there's hope. Our church for these four years is focused on "Jesus the Hope"—what a timely, timeless truth!

I do believe prayer is significant. I think that we've got to do more than just think of new ways. We've got to know why we do what we do. I think that's the importance of Ps. 122—the invitation to come to the house of God—it's a place of safety and refuge and worship. It's where people go to give thanks to the Lord. It's a place for hearing truth. And it's a place of prayer. I just believe that we need to let the church be the Church. The world at its worst needs the Church at its best.

I don't know that I have any magic formula or response except that I don't think that we've ever been given a greater opportunity than right now.

Are you confident that the Church will rise to this opportunity?

I come from a certain history and time, and I

was pretty young during the days of World War II. I've heard family members talk about it. I've heard other people talk about it. When the world was experiencing its toughest times, the Church was experiencing its greatest time.

Again we recognize our need to depend on God. Times have changed with technology—the same CNN that we're watching, Osama Bin Laden is watching—if he's still alive! Wherever we meet and greet people, we should not be filled with anxiety but express confidence in the midst of the storm. I think we've got to give it our best.

People are returning to church to find meaning, to find some answer. People who do not comprehend the sovereignty of God are saying, "How can these things be? Is this a loving God?" Why? The world is shifting. There are very few absolute points of reference. They're searching. I think we've got to be there with reality.

Dr. Jerry D. Porter

Dr. Porter expressed his gratitude for the unprecedented outpouring of generosity to the innocent victims of the attacks, as well as those who suffer in Afghanistan. Nazarenes have contributed over $700,000—the largest amount ever for a disaster offering.

What should the continuing response of Nazarenes be?

We rejoice to hear of the generous response of the Nazarene family to the 9/11 victims and their families. We honor those brave and dedicated Nazarene volunteers who have become the Good Samaritan to hurting members of our extended family. Beyond the practical response to physical needs, we now need to pray for those affected by this senseless tragedy. Pray for those who grieve the loss of loved ones, the loss of employment, the loss of innocence, and the loss of security. The grief process is unique to each individual. It takes God's grace and time to process the emotional roller coaster that follows a sad event like this. Those who are able to offer the compassionate ministry of presence—just being there—will be used of God as a means of healing grace to the affected ones.

How should life change when threatened by terrorism and the war against terrorism?

We will never be the same. We will learn to take new precautions to protect ourselves and those we love from this faceless threat. We will learn to go on living, by the grace of God, realizing that the Lord is with us, regardless of the situation that we may face. We will learn to weep with those who weep, and we will learn to forgive those who with evil intent invaded our cozy, safe world. We will learn to trust God all the more as life becomes more insane and complicated.

Should an international church address global economic inequities that many see as a contributing cause of terrorism?

The Church of God, and the Church of the Nazarene in particular, cannot ignore the injustice of global economic inequities that to some degree spur social, political, and terrorist unrest. As radical disciples of Jesus, we do not return an eye for an eye. We do not become bitter, nor do we play the victim and just point blame at others. Holy simplicity and generosity—making compassionate ministry a lifestyle—are a personal and family response to these pressing needs. As a church, we must find ways to confront injustice and evil at the personal and systemic levels. The Lord's greatest anger seethed against the legalistic religious persons and those who abused the religious system for their personal gain. The Lord's wrath will fall on us if we live our lives based on greed and avarice. We are called to be more than selfish consumers. We are called to be sensitive, generous, prophetic Good Samaritans. May God help us!

Dr. James H. Diehl

Some religious leaders have suggested that the terrorist attacks on 9/11 were the result of God's judgment on America. In this conversation, Dr. James H. Diehl reflects on this notion and the implications of terrorist activity for the Church and Nazarenes worldwide.

Where were you on 9/11?

I was at a pastors and spouses retreat on the West Texas District. It started on Monday night and was scheduled to go through Wednesday noon.

How did the persons attending respond?

We didn't have the normal nine o'clock meeting on Tuesday morning. Word was passed that everybody should hold steady. We gathered in the chapel at about eleven o'clock. They didn't want to do anything but get on their knees to pray and call out to God. I mean, it was a prayer meeting like I haven't heard in 40 years. It was real intense and intercessory praying.

What are the distinctive responses from the Wesleyan-Holiness perspective?

I don't believe that we Wesleyan-Holiness people should view such events as God's judgment on America or on New Yorkers or on anybody. When terrorists train and plan and get into airplanes and fly them into buildings, I don't believe God has a thing to do with that as far as causing that to happen. I think it's the result of terrible choices by sinful people.

We clearly believe that people everywhere are free moral agents. They made choices, and we have suffered. I strongly feel that we Wesleyan-Holiness people cannot jump up and say, "Well, God is bringing judgment because of this or that or the other." I just don't believe that.

How should Nazarenes respond to the event itself?

We must focus on Jesus rather than Satan. We must focus on forgiveness rather than revenge. We must focus on compassion to the victims rather than damnation to the criminals. We must focus on hope through Jesus rather than retribution from Almighty God.

Does the message of perfect love instruct us?

It does. The message of perfect love involves forgiveness. Not only that we have been forgiven and then cleansed and filled with the love of God in our hearts, but that, in turn, enables us to forgive people who have wronged us.

I'm quick to say that sometimes coming to a point of forgiveness is not instantaneous. It takes us awhile. It takes awhile to pray, to cry, to pour out our intense hurts because of all that has happened. But the grace of God is powerful enough to enable us to forgive people who have hurt us and wronged us, if we will just absolutely let the power and love of God work within our hearts and lives.

What is the message in this to the global church as well as to the U.S. church?

This was the worst terrorist attack ever for Americans. However, in many areas of the world, there are terrorist attacks of some nature every day. Now 9/11 is a date we will never forget, but just two days ago (March 27), a suicide bomber in Israel killed 19 people. It made the front page but will be forgotten in three days over here.

Terrorist attacks are not very common here. That's why we are doing all that we are doing. But it's a daily event in many places around the world. People around the world have to be ready to meet Jesus because they don't know what's going to happen on any given day.

As a global leader in a global church, you seem to be calling on Nazarenes to be global Christians.

True! We say that we are global Christians, and we are trying to be. We send Work and Witness teams to help people in other parts of the world to know that we really care. But it's very difficult for us Americans to really understand the global situation until we walk in no-man's-land, as I did recently, going from the Democratic Republic of the Congo to Rwanda at sundown. We were hurrying because there was danger at hand. Gunfire had just broken out in front of the church where the assembly was held, and they were trying to get me out of there. We were walking fast, trying to get across no-man's land and get to the other country.

Then it comes a little closer. "Man, this is dangerous, and these people live in that every day!"

We have thousands of Nazarenes that live in such danger every day. I know our American Nazarenes really want to empathize and to care. Therefore we just have to hear about it more to understand that that's where our people are.

How should American Nazarenes display their hope and faith?

We must do more than wave the American flag. I believe that as Christians and as Nazarenes we must wave high the bloodstained banner of Jesus Christ. On that banner, instead of stars and stripes, it has a cross and spilled blood. I'm an American, and I have a flag decal in the back window of my car. But my hope is not in the Stars and Stripes. It's in the banner of Jesus Christ. That I really do believe!

Dr. Paul G. Cunningham

How do Christians reconcile God's control with human freedom, and how should the Church respond to those who use their freedom to espouse hatred? In this conversation, Dr. Paul G. Cunningham reflects on the Christian response to hate and violence after the events of 9/11.

Where were you on 9/11?

I was at home making final preparations to leave to speak at a pastor and spouse retreat for the North Arkansas District. I headed for my office here at Nazarene Headquarters, where we began to put together a statement and to check with our missionary situation around the world and do the kinds of things that one needs to do with an international emergency.

How has your work been affected by 9/11?

We were traveling again within a matter of a few days following the tragedy because work does have to go on. As so many have said, "We can't surrender everything to the terrorists and allow them to change our lives." However, in fact, we all know that things aren't quite the same as they were. It's a bit daunting going through airports feeling like you and about a dozen other people are the only ones there except the National Guard and the police dogs. But after those first few flights, it seemed better. We did think it over on the international flight we took in October. That was the first out-of-the-country flight we had taken since 9/11, and we thought about all the things one thinks about under those circumstances.

How do you explain an event like this?

I think it is best explained by simply understanding the awesome power of choice that God gives to us. A loving God has given us incredible freedom as individuals to make choices and to face the consequences of those choices.

He does allow us enormous freedom, and as a result, people sometimes choose to make very bad choices. The power of evil is awesome, and occasionally it escalates to new heights. I think we saw a magnification of the power of evil unleashed on that day.

God has used it for good, just as He has promised to work in everything that happens to us to bring good out of it if we love Him and are called according to His purpose (see Rom. 8:28).

Is that the message that you encourage our pastors to convey to people who are coming to church with questions?

It is, because we believe that is what the Bible teaches. Throughout biblical times, terrible things happened from time to time and people suffered greatly. In the era of the Early Church, terrible things happened to Christians. But God has wonderfully worked in the lives of His people. We have climbed out every time.

I just returned from Russia, where I had the exciting privilege of ordaining the first three elders in the history of the Church of the Nazarene in Russia. I stood in Red Square. I grew up at the time of World War II and then on into the Cold War era. I can remember as a young person seeing Red Square in Moscow and seeing those intercontinental ballistic missiles being paraded through Red Square on May Day followed by those awesome tanks and the troops and the leaders of Russia in the reviewing stand. The whole world wondered what awful thing was going to come of all this.

And then, just a few days ago, I stood in Red Square in front of that reviewing stand, which happens to be Lenin's tomb. I thought to myself, "Lenin, you and your cohorts did everything you possibly could to crush the Church of Jesus Christ, to exterminate it. But here I am, a holiness preacher, and the reason I am here today is because in a little while I am going to be ordaining the first three elders in the Church of the Nazarene in Russia. You failed; you failed miserably. The Church of Jesus Christ still stands and not even the gates of hell can prevail against it." So I think this is our message for times past, times present, and the future.

What is it that causes people to be willing to commit suicide in order to kill other people?

An issue of *USA Today* came out during the general assembly last June. They had done some research with a terrorist group and saw how they took the children, teaching them to hate, nurturing them, growing up a crop of terrorists until by the time they are in their later teens all they have ever known is hatred and violence and that this is pleasing to God. These young people, with explosives strapped to their chests, annihilate themselves as well as whomever else they can in a demonstration of the power of combining education with high motivation. And the hatred provides the motivation. The education gives them the know-how as to how to exploit their hatred in the most destructive way possible.

Well, it doesn't take much to move that over to the Church. Love is also a very powerful emotion. When you take children and nurture them in the Word of God and in the power of His love and teach them how to exploit that love to achieve uncommon good, you have exactly the opposite effect [from hatred]. That, of course, is what the Church has been called to do with its love.

Is love the primary response to hatred?

It has to be. It is the only antidote to hatred. We have a responsibility all over the world to show the love of Jesus Christ in powerful ways. The most powerful demonstration always is the power of personal witness.

Grieving

PART 2

Reflections from Ground Zero

Tom Nees

The TV images of Ground Zero did not convey the gruesome reality of destruction, death, and despair in New York City following 9/11. On the Saturday following that fateful Tuesday, I joined with a group of Nazarene pastors in a high-rise Manhattan law firm. We were there for a teleconferencing training seminar on how to deal with trauma. Those New York pastors knew that they would be called upon to provide answers as well as comfort on Sunday. What does one say in the face of this sort of devastation?

Early Sunday morning I walked from the Lamb's Church of the Nazarene in Times Square several miles south to Ground Zero. Mere words cannot adequately describe the disbelief, fear, and anger of the people at Ground Zero. They couldn't believe the burning mountain of debris, the search for thousands of missing persons, the shattered confidence of a city no longer invulnerable.

Nazarene leaders and volunteers were at Ground Zero—and are still working today with and through Nazarene Disaster Response. They have served thousands of needy and sometimes traumatized neighbors and friends.

Immediately after 9/11, contributions began to arrive. In the year following, Nazarenes have contributed over $700,000 that has been more than matched by outside cash and donations of food, clothing, and emergency supplies.

The Metro New York District and more than 100 churches and missions became a network of relief resources. District Superintendent Dr. Dallas Mucci made it his personal responsibility to support and comfort the pastors who would become the frontline caregivers in the years following 9/11. Dr. J. V. Morsch, national NDR coordinator, came immediately to organize the largest disaster effort ever undertaken in the United States. The local disaster committee asked Rev. Brian Kido to delay his mission of starting a new church in order to direct the relief effort.

They were there, and through these abbreviated reflections they provide a glimpse of Ground Zero.

Volunteers unload donations at local shelter

Through the Smoking Disaster

> *9/11 Reflections from*
> *Dr. Dallas D. Mucci*
> *District Superintendent,*
> *Metro New York District*

On the morning of 9/11, my studies were interrupted by a phone call. It was a friend from Florida with a question I'll never forget, "What's going on at the World Trade Center?"

"Business as usual . . . " Before I could finish, he stopped me—"A plane has crashed into a tower of the World Trade Center, according to the TV I'm watching." I dropped the phone and rushed to my own television. We live too far north to have seen the twin towers.

With sickening horror I watched growing flames licking their way around the tower. I had to hang up; we would talk later. I rushed to my office, feeling utterly helpless as I thought of Nazarenes who worked in the massive World Trade Center Plaza. My prayer was a garbled request for God's help! God answered in many ways, especially through our fellow Nazarenes here and across our nation and around the world.

I learned too quickly that fireman Bruce Van Hine from our Warwick Church was missing, and we

Dr. Dallas Mucci

now know he died heroically trying to save others. What about Javier Garcia, bivocational pastor of Bayside Queens—I remembered his office was up high in one of the towers. The next day I learned that he had been transferred uptown just a short time earlier and thus missed the disaster. In the following days, the stories of rescue, escape, death, and the resulting human and spiritual need galvanized our Metro New York District Nazarenes into action.

God's answer through these Nazarenes is typified by these few antidotes from the many. More than 50 percent of the churches were quickly involved in individual and cooperative ministry across our shattered city.

Bivocational Pastor Ray Greene of our Middletown Church was on his way to the Trade Center to secure communications equipment for a company project in Manhattan and was fortuitously delayed, thus saved from the collapse of the Twin Towers. He became a spectator to the fire, fully aware of the communication disaster that had occurred. There were more communication systems in those towers than in the entire city of Detroit, and the systems were now destroyed.

Pastor Ray was a key cell phone expert in his small company. Verizon, the eastern communication giant, called for help and Ray was the lead man sent to grapple with this desperate need. It was critical to establish communication in the fire and smoke to assist with rescue efforts.

Rev. Ray Greene

Climbing atop the tallest buildings not directly impacted by the mighty explosion, Ray attempted to connect the cell systems by the electronic beams. But they would not penetrate the smoke. All attempts had failed.

A break in the smoke appeared, and Ray was able to get a signal through the smoke and establish the link. He praised God, and workers were empowered by this breakthrough. He spent a month of 12- to 15-hour days assisting in keeping cell phone communications open. Then, suddenly, his company went bankrupt, and he was out of work.

But God answered again as Nazarenes across America gave so generously, and the local Nazarene Disaster Response (NDR) committee assisted the Greenes with essentials until he secured a new job.

Rev. Errol Vieira, pastor of Queens Ozone Park Church, is the local NDR director for Metro New York. He connected with Dr. J. V. Morsch, national NDR director, and they began building a structure to marshal Nazarene efforts and cooperate with all other agencies in spiritual and compassionate ministry to the city.

Rev. Vieira led a group of Nazarenes into the streets of Manhattan to counsel and pray with those stricken by the loss of loved ones and friends in the early days of the disaster. They prayed with the hundreds cloistered around the makeshift memorials in the city streets.

A hotline was established at the Manhattan Lamb's Church, and the volume of calls of offers to help and calls requesting help quickly overwhelmed the staff. Rev. Vieira, a bivocational pastor, was also stretched beyond capacity. Again, God answered.

Rev. Brian Kido had just come to New York to assist in the planting of a new Japanese-speaking church. He was asked by Pastor John Bowen of the Lamb's to help in the overload at the Lamb's. In this crunch, the NDR committee discovered that Brian was especially gifted for this work. The Metro District granted a delay in the Japanese new start until summer.

Christian Camping International heard of the Nazarene effort. They covered the cost of full summer camp scholarships for 100 children directly or indirectly affected by the WTC Disaster at Camp

Taconic, our Nazarene Center near Red Hook, New York. Several hundred thousand dollars were given by other groups to match the NDR efforts coordinated by Rev. Kido.

Rev. Vieira continued to work closely with the local Nazarene churches and was the key person to coordinate meeting the immediate needs of Nazarenes affected by the attacks. He was invaluable in assisting our churches to become centers where food, clothing, and medical supplies could be distributed to needy members and the surrounding community.

Nazarene pastors trained by the Red Cross and those with prior counseling training worked at Ground Zero with families, policemen, and firemen. Pastor David Verzyl of the Kingston Church, as an example, served several nights a week for months as a chaplain in the morgue at Ground Zero. All of these were greatly assisted by the prayer and financial support of Nazarenes across America.

Brooklyn Bridge

Ground Zero

Grace Brathwaite

God answered as the stunned Brooklynites walking up Washington Avenue after the long trek across the Brooklyn Bridge were met with cups of cold water by the staff of Hope City, compassionate ministry center of the Brooklyn Beulah Church. Hope City became a counseling center on September 11.

NDR gave a significant grant to Hope City that was matched by World Relief. Those grants birthed a counseling program that continues to help those suffering from post-traumatic stress. Grace Brathwaite of Brooklyn Beulah Church and Dr. Miriam Azaunce of Community Worship Center Church organized and lead the team of volunteers and professionals.

Thousands will be touched in Christ's name because Nazarenes cared enough to give.

Mourning

The suffering and pain from this tragedy still haunt our daily lives. Sometimes it seems more difficult now, a year later, than during the hectic early days of search and clean up. Metro New York pastors have become frontline troops. They have quit asking why and have given themselves as lavish expressions of God's grace. Whatever was called for, our Nazarenes have had strength given by the Holy Spirit to give. Those at the epicenter of the devastating blast are still faithfully serving!

Metro New York Nazarenes thank our fellow Nazarenes for contributions of cash and supplies and volunteering to help New York City pick up the broken pieces. Please pray with us for a spiritual awakening. The physical rebuilding of the city will come. The spiritual needs are now our compelling concern.

Serving at Ground Zero

Reflections from Brian Kido
On-Site Disaster Coordinator

I had just dropped my wife off at work. After turning on the radio, I noticed something was different—terribly different. There was no music, no commercials, and certainly no jokes. All the radio announcers were dead serious about what had just happened a few moments earlier—the 9/11 World Trade Center Terrorist Attacks. In fact, they were so serious that it was the "potential dead" they were talking about. As I rushed home, I jumped out of my car, ran in the house, and then turned on the TV. I couldn't believe my eyes as I watched all the smoke, fire, and two planes crashing into the Twin Towers. I knew, without a doubt, that my life would never be the same.

In the months since the attacks, I reflected on Ps. 46:1, "God is our refuge and strength, a very present help in trouble" (KJV). It was this strength and presence that gave me hope through the dark, gloomy clouds that hovered over so many for so long.

The Church of the Nazarene, through Nazarene Disaster Response (NDR), has indeed heard the cry of all of the victims in the Metro New York City area and surrounding communities. We have the task

Rev. Brian Kido

of not only supplying the material needs of the people but also reaching hearts that have become so fragile since the 9/11 attacks.

During the first several months, I received nearly 100 calls every day. Hundreds of people from all over the United States. called to offer help. Others only wanted an update. Still others wanted to make donations of money or goods—food, water, chocolate, and even teddy bears—anything to make a difference. They were ready to send hundreds of boxes of goods; but where would we store them? The situation became more and more complicated.

NDR worked with the Red Cross, The Salvation Army, FEMA, International AID, World Relief, Heart-to-Heart, the Manhattan Lamb's Church of the Nazarene, and many other organizations. Our goal was to work together to meet the needs of those in trouble.

Here is a partial list of the ways that Nazarenes

through Nazarene Disaster Response has been helping during the year after 9/11.

- The Lamb's Church of the Nazarene in Manhattan continues to use its building in Manhattan to provide housing for volunteer disaster workers. Many individuals and Christian organizations have been utilizing the Lamb's Church as a base for reaching the 9/11 victims with love and compassion.
- NDR has been working directly with FEMA, the Red Cross, and The Salvation Army. These organizations refer individuals in need to us. Others come to us directly.
- Through NDR we have helped victims with financial assistance. This aid could be in the form of paying the monthly rent or monthly mortgage payment of unemployed individuals who lost jobs due to the 9/11 disaster. Sometime it

Volunteers help unload donated supplies

is something as urgent as providing grocery money for a family who may be waiting for a late check to come in. We consider each request seriously and act as quickly as possible.

- NDR has been a resource center for various organizations that are in need of information such as finding volunteers, distributing thank-you cards to firemen, looking for organizations to receive clothes for victims of 9/11.

"Jesus Christ Eternal Ministries" contacted NDR for help in distributing $591,436.11 worth of new clothes. They could not accomplish this task alone. They needed help. Within a few hours all the clothes were distributed to the 9/11 victims and workers at Ground Zero through NDR's partnership with The Salvation Army.

- NDR has provided counseling for those who were unable to pay personal bills. There are many people who do not want money but simply want some direction on how they can put their 9/11 situations into "words that make sense," so perhaps they could get an extension on a payment or a decrease in final payment. NDR has helped numerous individuals such as these over the phone. And we have also received calls and letters with words of thanks. Many people tried contacting other organizations for help without much success prior to contacting NDR; they thought it was a dead end. But NDR gave them hope to try once more with a different approach—and it worked! NDR could not help everyone, but we did make a big difference.

- NDR has worked with the Lamb's Church in helping the families who lost their jobs as a result of the 9/11 disaster. A Christmas Store at the Lamb's Church during the Christmas season provided 9/11 victims with Christmas gifts, toys, care kits, and winter clothing. The line to the Christmas Store extended outside for more than a block. Many individuals and families asked for prayer. They needed to talk and pray about their grief and suffering. The Lamb's Easter Store was equally successful in reaching the needs of 9/11 victims looking for hope in a time of need.

All of us on the Metro New York District representing the Church of the Nazarene through Nazarene Disaster Response appreciate the prayer and support of Nazarenes in the year after 9/11. We'll continue to meet the needs of 9/11 victims for as long as necessary.

Volunteers delivering supplies

Thanks to a Generous Church

9/11 Reflections from J. V. Morsch
National NDR Field Director

We now reflect—and remember—one year later. Volunteers and donors weep for people they don't know, pray for people they haven't met, and support people they've never seen. Volunteers and donors are rebuilding lives rather than rebuilding buildings. They are giving hope and encouragement to the affected families and victims of the 9/11 New York and Pentagon tragedies and to the families who lost their heroic loved ones in the plane tragedy near Shanksville, Pennsylvania.

Out of the tons of debris at Ground Zero, a worker found a huge steel-beam cross that had fallen from a World Trade Center Tower into a nearby building. Against the backdrop of a large waving American flag, the workers erected this perfectly untouched symmetrical cross as a memorial.

Following the attack, the Hope City Empowerment Compassion Center at the Brooklyn Beulah Church of the Nazarene was New York's first volunteer faith group to respond to the thousands of victims running for their lives across the Brooklyn Bridge from Ground Zero. The Center is only a few blocks away from the legendary bridge crossing. Director Grace Brathwaite saw the despair on those victims' faces as they ran for safety and knew they had to do something. And they did! Although nearly 3,000 lost their lives, thousands of others fled the collapsing towers.

Dr. J. V. Morsch

By the end of the day on 9/11, the Manhattan Lamb's Church of the Nazarene in Times Square a few miles north of Ground Zero was designated the NDR disaster center. This historic ministry center was already highly respected in the city. Metro New York District Superintendent Dallas Mucci, Lamb's Pastor John Bowen and his staff, NDR District Director Errol Vieira, and Disaster Director Rev. Brian Kido were already responding with effective leadership. Many of the Metro New York District's 130 churches and missions were already opening their doors for prayer and consolation to their communities. Volunteers from across the nation came to help.

When United Airlines Flight 93 crashed in the field 80 miles southeast of Pittsburgh, Randy Dillow and the Boswell, Pennsylvania, New Life Church of the Nazarene volunteers immediately responded, assisting the emergency response teams.

By September 15, Metro New York NDR District

Director Rev. Errol Vieira had organized teams to bring hope and prayer to the thousands of people who visited the temporary memorial centers that were set up in the city parks. Hundreds of pictures were posted in memory of loved ones, and candles burned night and day. The mourners were open to prayer and consolation. Ten thousand CD's of "In God's Hands" were distributed. Our volunteers helped pass out 25 million copies of Campus Crusade's *Fallen But Not Forgotten* 16-page book. People stood in line to accept a complimentary copy. Many were open to accepting the Lord as their Savior.

NDR Disaster Director Brian Kido also linked up with Youth-With-a-Mission's "Prayer Stations" throughout the massive subway system in New York City and the Boroughs.

Among the many church families who lost friends and relatives at Ground Zero and at the Pentagon are the families of lay leaders Edward Rowenhorst and Bruce Van Hine. These bereaved families are a great witness to the grace of God. Traci Rowenhurst and her two daughters attend the Fredericksburg, Virginia, Salem Fields Community Church of the Nazarene. Edward was a civilian accountant for the United States Army at the Pentagon. Bruce Van Hine, a fireman from Squad 41, lost his life working at Ground Zero. Ann Van Hine and her two daughters are members of the Warrick Valley, New York, Church of the Nazarene. Because Ann Van Hine's husband was a fireman, the Fire Chief asked her to share her testimony in

Ground Zero

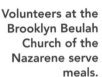
Volunteers at the Brooklyn Beulah Church of the Nazarene serve meals.

many New York City fire stations, giving witness to the saving and sustaining grace of God, emphasizing "His Grace Is Sufficient."

The Metro New York churches reached out in creative and supportive ways. Special tribute services were held in the home churches of firefighters, policemen, or emergency workers. Rev. John Borgal of Nazarene Compassionate Ministries transported in 2,500 crisis care kits from the Pennsylvania warehouse within days.

From the very beginning, when the Pentagon's Survivors Assistance Center notified us of needs or New York's Emergency Command Center at Pier 90 gave referrals, Nazarenes were there. The NDR directors, with the help of the local disaster committee members Rev. Darren Ojeda, Rev. Jan Rizzon, Cindy DuPree, Rev. John Bowen, Karen Shelton, and Jennifer Osborn, went the second mile to make this response possible.

They cooperated with the government Emergency Operation Command Center and the VOAD (Volunteer Organizations Active in Disaster Response) groups, which include FEMA, the American Red Cross, The Salvation Army, and many recognized faith and humanitarian disaster response groups.

Rev. John Bowen and the Manhattan Lamb's Ministry Center staff graciously opened their doors to Nazarene Disaster Response allowing the facility to be used as the NDR disaster headquarters. They worked diligently in the distribution of supplies, rehabilitation, counseling, and training.

Gerald Smith interviews John Bowen on Times Square.

From the Lamb's, NDR collaborates daily with Campus Crusade for Christ, Youth-With-a-Mission, Heart-to-Heart International, International Aid, World Relief, Christian Church Disaster

Volunteers delivering supplies

Response, Billy Graham Prayer Center, Willing Hearts, FEMA, Association of Police Chaplains, and the American Red Cross. Nyack College's New York Campus faculty and student body used the Center for regrouping and planning following the temporary closure of their campus near Ground Zero.

Nazarene college and university volunteer student groups, Work and Witness teams, and Nazarenes in Volunteer Service recruited and direct hundreds of volunteers. It has been and continues to be "one family" working together. Even the New York City Mayor's Office "limousine service" came by to escort General Superintendent Jesse Middendorf and other NDR leaders to Ground Zero!

Heart-to-Heart International donated space in a Brooklyn warehouse so that NDR could store support supplies and personal hygiene kits, allowing NDR to provide donated food, supplies, and over-the-counter medicines for the church's distribution and compassionate centers. Recently 91,000 tasty "MRE's" (Meals Ready to Eat) were delivered to the warehouse for distribution. Support supplies have come from as far away as Oregon and as close as the world's largest Toys R Us in Times Square. Several semitrailer loads of much-needed items came from locations around the country and will continue . . . all going "beyond the call."

NDR's National Crisis Counselor Director Dr. Phil Budd from Southern Nazarene University, a veteran of the Oklahoma City bombing response, immediately set up plans to have a telecommunication conference, instructing pastors, lay leaders, and disaster response workers in the New York area on basic steps to help those impacted by trauma. Dr. Jan Lanham, Eastern Nazarene College, also a Ph.D. in Trauma Counseling, assisted in the two conference locations. The Bell South and the Times Square Conference Center donated the $250,000 teleconference cost.

In early February, Camp Taconic became the setting for further renewal and support for pastors and spouses on the front line. Again, Dr. Jesse Middendorf uplifted and encouraged the pastoral leaders working in recovery. Dr. Al Truesdale gave theological support and distributed complimentary copies of his book "If God Is God, Then Why?" Dr. Harold Ivan Smith, a well-known grief counselor, offered sound support for healthy grieving. During the week of September 11, the Nazarene Publishing House sent complimentary copies of Dr. Smith's books, "When Your People Are Grieving" and "A Decembered Grief" to every pastor on the Metro New York and Washington, D.C., districts.

Ground Zero

This timely retreat provided additional strength and understanding for the future. Other gatherings will be held in the future to combat compassion fatigue and to support the district as it continues to lead in recovery.

The Metro New York District's Camp Taconic is hosting children's camps for families victimized by the 9/11 attack. Professional children's counselors will participate in the activities scheduled throughout the summer. Other retreats are being planned for recovery support volunteers.

A year ago the world gathered around television sets to watch the horror of terrorism. Four passenger jets departed within 42 minutes of one another from three East Coast airports. The planes were transformed by hijackers into fuel-laden missiles. Two pierced the Twin Towers in New York City and another rammed into the Pentagon building in Washington, D.C. The fourth crashed in a field near Shanksville, Pennsylvania.

Along with many others, I happened to walk by a television set at 9:02 A.M. and caught a glimpse of the plane hitting the South Tower. The agony of watching people jump from windows on the upper floors of the Towers and the frequent reruns of the Towers collapsing is forever etched in our minds. Not only will the world never be the same again, but also you and I will probably never be the same.

Nazarenes didn't turn inward and shut out the pain of the world. We have allowed these events to be instruments of growth for our hearts and minds as we reach out to those in need with deeper compassion and love.

The response is unprecedented. More than $700,000 has been given through the Church of the Nazarene for victim support, and this amount has been matched in direct financial support, goods, and services from others.

One year later, the church continues to respond with compassion in Jesus' name.

NDR volunteers pray with victims' families.

Waiting

Firefighter at Ground Zero.

Lighting candles in memory.

PART 3

Through the Lens
Larger than Life!
9/11 Reflections from
Gerald Smith
Director, Premier Studios

As part of the Nazarene Disaster Response, the call came from Nazarene Communications Network to get a camera crew to New York to document the stories and images surrounding the 9/11 tragedy. At first I was hesitant to go. I could not clear my thoughts of the images we had seen just hours before on television. How would the city and our country be able to respond to a disaster of such magnitude?

Scott Stearman, a producer at Premier Studios, and I booked the next available flight to New York City. As I prepared for our trip, I found myself consumed with the question, "How do we as Christians respond?" New York City seemed so far removed from Kansas City. I had been there numerous times on business. Just months before, my wife, Dianna, and I had stood atop the World Trade Center and snapped a photo that would now become one our most treasured photographs.

Ground Zero

Boarding the plane to New York City with all our video equipment just days after the tragedy was ironically easier than it would be a year later with so much increased security. I spent the flight trying to imagine what I would see and preparing myself. I was reserved—looking through a camera lens can be larger than life, and stir emotions that can sometimes scar. To my surprise, our plane flew directly over Ground Zero on the approach to La Guardia Airport. It looked as though the earth had opened up, and steam and smoldering ash were coming out of its center. I might have guessed that a meteor had hit the middle of Manhattan. I will never forget that image.

We hit the ground running. The greatest blessing of the trip met us at the airport—his friends call him "Joe-the-Cop" (or as they say in New York City, "Joe-da-Cop"). His real name is Joe Radecki, a retired New York City police officer, who seemed to know just about everyone in New York City personally. Joe spent most of our trip getting us into places that would otherwise have been impossible to access. His familiarity with the city and its traffic, along with his understanding of what this tragedy would mean to New Yorkers allowed us to squeeze six days of shooting into three. Cindy Dupree, the on-site NCN reporter, and David Best, of Towel & Basin Ministries, accompanied us during some of the shooting.

Joe-da-Cop

We interviewed person after person, all telling their own story of how they responded on 9/11. There were people such as Ray Greene, who was helping reestablish communi-

Wenton Fyne and Grace Brathwaite ministering at Brooklyn Beulah Church of the Nazarene.

Elizabeth Choi, wife of firefighter Jerry Choi

cations at Ground Zero; Pastor Tom Saunders, who was counseling with survivors and their families, as well as victims' families; Wenton Fyne & Grace Brathwaite of the Brooklyn Beulah Church of the Nazarene, who opened their doors in compassion to the survivors that were flooding across the Brooklyn Bridge, moments after the tragedy; New York City firefighter Jerry Choi, who after spending multiple shifts at Ground Zero, took a brief break the following Saturday to keep an appointment at the altar. Only hours after his wedding Jerry was back on duty, part of the rescue effort. Everywhere we went, Nazarenes had wonderful stories like these.

We visited countless makeshift memorials, mostly located in city parks or near fire stations. Thousands of flowers, candles, and notes to loved-ones, many of these from people who only came to share in the grieving process. We talked to as many people as time would allow. Everyone knew someone who had been impacted by this tragedy.

After much maneuvering around the city and numerous phone calls to friends, Joe-the-Cop had found a way to Ground Zero. We would approach from the south end where the trucks were coming and going from the site. On the way we passed the location where the debris was being loaded onto barges and being taken to the landfill for processing. At the south entrance of the site I was overwhelmed by the enormity of the debris. It was then I fully realized that I had stood atop these huge buildings on numerous occasions. Their metal and concrete had fallen onto the area I was now seeing. Words cannot describe the enormity of the catastrophe. What we see on television is a two-dimensional view. In person, you realize there is depth and width and height to all this debris. It was hard to take in, over 16 acres of devastation.

Lighting Candles in remembrance

Seeing the devastation of the site firsthand connected all the statements from interviews that we had heard over the two days prior. I couldn't imagine how those who responded dealt with such catastrophe and the resulting sorrow. Yet all those we had come in contact with were each being used in a specific way by God.

I will ever be thankful for the opportunity to be in New York City those few days. My faith was strengthened. My hope for the Church of the Nazarene was charged, and my thankfulness for this great country was renewed. I'm reminded of an interview with a man named Stephen Connolly, who said, "For a brief moment on 9/11, every freedom loving person in the world became an American and every American became a New Yorker."

Paying tribute

Rescue worker at Ground Zero

Ground Zero

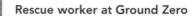

Writing notes to
loved ones.

Patriotism

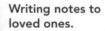

Firefighter at Ground Zero

Lighting candles in remembrance.

Ground Zero

Patriotism

Rescuers sift through the wreckage at Ground Zero.

Ground Zero

Paying tribute to victims.

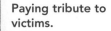

American Flag displayed near Ground Zero.

Ground Zero

Visitors to the
memorials in local
parks write notes
to victims missing
in the tragedy.

The NYC skyline

Memorial to FDNY
victims.